GOD'S LITTLE BOOK OF GUARANTEES

LITTLE BOOKS FOR MARRIAGE

HEATHER KOPP

Multnomah®Publishers *Sisters, Oregon*

GOD'S LITTLE BOOK OF GUARANTEES FOR MARRIAGE
published by Multnomah Publishers, Inc.
Published in association with the literary agency of Ann Spangler and Associates,
1420 Pontiac Road, S.E., Grand Rapids, Michigan 49506

© 2002 by Heather Kopp
International Standard Book Number: 1-59052-022-X

Cover image by Corbis

Unless otherwise indicated, Scripture quotations are the author's own paraphrase
Other Scripture quotations:
The Holy Bible, New King James Version (NKJV)
© 1984 by Thomas Nelson, Inc.
The Holy Bible, New International Version (NIV)
© 1973, 1984 by International Bible Society,
used by permission of Zondervan Publishing House

Multnomah is a trademark of Multnomah Publishers, Inc.,
and is registered in the U.S. Patent and Trademark Office.
The colophon is a trademark of Multnomah Publishers, Inc.

Printed in the United States of America

For information:
MULTNOMAH PUBLISHERS, INC. • P.O. Box 1720 • SISTERS, OR 97759

Library of Congress Cataloging-in-Publication Data

Kopp, Heather Harpham, 1964-
    God's little book of guarantees for marriage / by Heather Kopp.
        p. cm.
    ISBN 1-59052-022-X (pbk.)
    1. Marriage—Religious aspects—Christianity.   I. Title.
    BV835 .K67 2002
    242'.644—dc21

                                                    2002005825

02 03 04 05 06 07 08—10 9 8 7 6 5 4 3 2 1 0

Table of Contents

One

God's

Guarantees

about His

Love—and Yours

God Guarantees

YOU HAVE MY REDEEMING LOVE

Husband, wife, put your hope in Me. I am fail-safe, foolproof, as certain as sunrise and sunset. My love will *unfailingly* support and surround you—I guarantee it.

FROM PSALM 130:7

WARRANTY NOTES: IT'S A GUARANTEE THAT EMPOWERS YOUR OWN LOVING EVERY DAY: GOD'S LOVE REDEEMS YOURS.

Dear God,
I need to rely on Your perfect love more fully. My own love is so flawed and unsteady; please help me to know and express Your quality of care with my spouse today.
Thank You.
Amen.

God Guarantees

I FORGIVE, I BLESS,
I ABOUND IN LOVE
FOR YOU

My mercy and goodness are immeasurable—count on them! Know that when you call to Me, the love I feel for and express to you is deep, *beyond emptying.*

FROM PSALM 86:5

WARRANTY NOTES: FORGIVENESS FOR FAILURE, AFFECTION FOR NEEDINESS—WHAT A WONDROUS EXCHANGE!

Dear God,
I'm so grateful for the gifts You give. Thank You
especially today for Your mercy. I rest in it today—and I
offer it to my spouse just as You offer it to me.
Amen.

God Guarantees

YOUR LOVE CAN GROW

My servant Paul prayed for you! He asked that your love would abound as you grew in knowledge and insight. Husband or wife, I empower Paul's prayer and see every effort you make to fulfill your potential as My disciple. Know that I will increase your love—for each other, for Me, for others—as you seek Me.

FROM PHILIPPIANS 1:9

WARRANTY NOTES: LOVE'S SUPPLY IS DEPENDENT ON LOVE'S SOURCE: GOD.

Dear God,
I long, with Paul, to see my love expand and enrich those I care for—including You. Please continue to help me grow, to Your glory and to the blessing of those in my family, especially my spouse.
Amen.

God Guarantees

I NEVER WITHHOLD MY LOVE FROM YOU

I hear you…I see you…I answer you. I never hide My love behind judgment or bury it under expectation. My love is simply yours: freely, fully, forever. Count on it.

FROM PSALM 66:20

WARRANTY NOTES: IT'S ODD HOW WE SOMETIMES RESERVE OUR LOVE FOR OTHERS BASED ON THEIR PERFORMANCE. IT'S AMAZING THAT GOD NEVER DOES THE SAME.

Dear God,
I am guilty of doling out love according to my
whims or whether my spouse pleases me.
Please forgive me for being stingy with something You
provide so richly. Today may I love You—
and my spouse—as You deserve.
Amen.

God Guarantees

FORGIVENESS
FOSTERS LOVE

When you forgive, you promote—encourage, put forward, honor—love. It's that simple. If you long to see abundant affection in your marriage relationship, overlook offenses. You will know the peace that comes from forgiveness bestowed often and completely—I guarantee it.

FROM PROVERBS 17:9; 10:12

WARRANTY NOTES: SO SIMPLE—BUT SO HARD! LOVE GROWS NATURALLY FROM THE SEEDS OF FREE FORGIVENESS.

Dear God,
I know the tender feelings that arise as I sense Your
acceptance of me, failures and all. I want to give my
spouse the opportunity to feel that same peace with me
so our love can grow. Empower us in this today.
Amen.

God Guarantees

LOVE AND PERSEVERANCE GO TOGETHER

To be effective, love must endure. Know that I am the source for these impossible dreams: I alone can ignite love and strengthen perseverance. Look to Me for the ability to do what you cannot, and you will have all you need.

FROM 2 THESSALONIANS 3:5

WARRANTY NOTES: HOW GOOD IT IS TO KNOW THAT ALL I CANNOT PRODUCE, GOD CAN— AND WILL!

Dear God,
My love is failing today.
Too many needs, too many demands, too little reserve.
I am dry. Please fill me with Your love and
Your endurance. Please fill my spouse also
so that we may serve You well.
Amen.

God Guarantees

LOVE IS STRONGER THAN ANYTHING!

No threat from within or without—disaster or doubt, pain or persecution—is any match for My love…or yours. The fact is, My love is a flame that knows no threat from water, even from flood. Count on this love to save you and to instill in you the love you need to serve your mate faithfully.

FROM SONGS OF SOLOMON 8:6–7

WARRANTY NOTES: NOTHING CAN QUENCH LOVE—NOT MANY WATERS, NOT FLOODS— NOR CAN MONEY PURCHASE IT.

Dear God,
I surrender to love today.
Rather than quelling it with unforgivingness
or hardness of heart, I give in.
Fill me with love that I may express
Your character this way.
Amen.

God Guarantees

I WILL HONOR EXPRESSIONS OF SINCERE LOVE

Don't bother with pretense—talking about love or making showy displays yet failing to actually love meaningfully. Love in theory is worthless; love in action is everything. Prove your claims to love your spouse by backing them up with kind words, an understanding heart, and profuse patience. I promise to honor and bless such activity!

FROM ROMANS 12:9

WARRANTY NOTES: GOD LOVES US IN WORD AND DEED—SO MUST WE LOVE EACH OTHER.

*Dear God, it's so much easier to say a quick
"love you" than to do it, but I want to.
Your example inspires me, Lord. Let me give You glory
by loving my spouse deeply, truly, actively.
Amen.*

God Guarantees

YOUR LOVE
GIVES ME JOY

Know that I see and applaud every effort you make to love your spouse. Your success gives Me great pleasure! Seeing the way you refresh each other's hearts is treasure to My eyes. Keep up the good work—I celebrate it!

FROM PHILEMON 1:7

WARRANTY NOTES: IT'S EASY TO ASSUME THAT GOD SEES ONLY OUR MISTAKES, NEVER OUR VICTORIES. THIS ISN'T TRUE! EVEN OUR FLAWED EFFORTS BRING JOY TO HIM.

Dear God,
I'm thankful that You see my energies to love and
that You cheer me on toward success in marriage.
I praise You for this twofold gift:
my marriage and Your help!
Amen.

Two

God's

Guarantees

about

Forgiveness

God Guarantees

FORGIVENESS
LEADS TO TRUST

Forgiveness finds its roots in Me. Because I forgive
your failures, you trust and fear Me. Where mercy
is withheld you find painful scrutiny, judgment,
and insecurity. Where mercy flows, love and faith
abound. Count on it.

FROM PSALM 130:4

WARRANTY NOTES: IT WORKS THIS WAY IN
MARRIAGE AS WELL: BECAUSE YOU EXTEND
MERCY TO EACH OTHER, A LIFE-GIVING SENSE
OF TRUST EXISTS BETWEEN YOU.

Dear God,
There are two things that we as a couple cannot do
without: forgiveness and trust. Help us to grow in both
and to know the richness of love that results.
Amen.

God Guarantees

THE QUALITY OF YOUR LOVE REFLECTS ME

Love each other in the way you have been loved by Me. Say kind words; act compassionately; forgive as I have forgiven you. Understand that these are the components of a godly marriage—this is behavior I honor! And rest assured that when you love this way, your marriage will become a picture of Me.

FROM EPHESIANS 4:32

WARRANTY NOTES: WE HAVE A GREAT EXAMPLE TO FOLLOW. LET US DO SO FAITH-FULLY.

Dear God,
I want to reflect Your flawless character in all I do. Help
me today to express kindness and forgiveness to my
spouse, that he or she may see You in me. Thank You
for empowering me to do all the good You command.
Amen.

God Guarantees

I Forgive
Hidden Sins

Husband and wives, you know that I forgive every sin you acknowledge. Today I want you to know that I also forgive the blind spots that hinder every person alive: the subconscious slights that you're not even aware you're committing. Yes, My forgiveness is that broad, as long as the sinner asks for it.

FROM PSALM 19:12

Warranty Notes: Whew! Even the wrongs I commit unknowingly can find coverage under God's vast mercy.

Dear God,
I praise You for Your mercy.
Cleanse me today of the errors I know I've made,
as well as those I'm unaware of.
Make me sensitive to all the ways
I can serve You better.
Amen.

God Guarantees

I WILL FORGIVE—
IF YOU WILL!

I will be glad to forgive you—as you forgive others who fail you. If you hoard My mercy, know that it will be limited. It grows only as you share it!

FROM MATTHEW 6:14–15

WARRANTY NOTES: GOD MEANS FOR FORGIVENESS TO FLOW LIKE THE OCEAN—IN AND OUT, CONTINUOUSLY.

Dear God,
I see myself in this Scripture.
I am often one who wants to receive forgiveness
without offering it to those around me, especially to
the one I love, and argue with, most: my spouse.
Forgive me and fill me with Your
mercy that I may share it.
Amen.

God Guarantees

FORGIVENESS PAVES A PRAYER PATH

Don't try to pray while you harbor resentment toward anyone. Instead, forgive your oppressor, and then you can know in your heart with all wonderful certainty that I will forgive you.

FROM MARK 11:25

WARRANTY NOTES: GOD WANTS YOUR CONVERSATION WITH HIM TO BE FREE OF DISTRACTIONS AND SECRETS. KEEP THE SIN OF UNFORGIVINGNESS OUT OF IT.

Dear God,
Today I confess that I am angry with my spouse for
_____. I don't want it to detract from my
relationship with You—or him or her. Please forgive me,
and help me to forgive as well. I need to have clear
channels of communication with You!
Amen.

God Guarantees

WALKING IN THE LIGHT MEANS WALKING IN FORGIVENESS

I have called you to walk in holiness—to walk with Me. When you do this, you share rich fellowship with your spouse—and with Me. The result? The blood of My Son, Jesus, washes away all your sin.

FROM 1 JOHN 1:7

WARRANTY NOTES: IT'S A WIN-WIN SITUATION: WALKING IN GOD'S WAYS MEANS A BLESSED MARRIAGE AS WELL AS A LIFE RICH IN MERCY.

Dear God,
I want to swim in Your mercy today.
Let Your light reveal every wicked way in me,
let Jesus' blood wash them away, and let Your
Spirit empower me to grow in righteousness.
Amen.

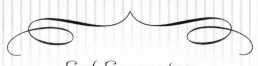

God Guarantees

FORGIVENESS PROVES YOU'RE MINE

If a man or woman claims to follow Me but does not obey my commands, such as forgiving others, you can tell that he or she is a liar. Walking in mercy, as I have commanded you and exemplified in Jesus, is important to Me. Be a shiningly authentic disciple in your marriage: Forgive, and I will make My love complete in you.

FROM 1 JOHN 2:4–6

WARRANTY NOTES: WE CAN'T BE FULL OF LOVE AND FULL OF GUILE; ONE HAS TO GO!

Dear God,
What a wonderful thought—
to see Your love fulfilled in me!
I want to cooperate with Your work in me. I forgive my
spouse today for the ways he/she has failed me, and I
seek Your forgiveness for the ways I've offended You.
Amen.

God Guarantees

HUMILITY LEADS
TO HONOR

Do you feel crushed today, pressed down and anchored by a hard heart and a scorecard weighted against your spouse? Humble yourself, and find yourself lifted up. Confess your sins, let your spouse confess his or hers, and discover the release that comes from grace. I will give it just when you need it most!

FROM 1 PETER 5:5–6

WARRANTY NOTES: HUMILITY PUTS US ALL ON EVEN GROUND BEFORE GOD. WHAT A RELIEF!

Dear God,
I confess today that I have kept score against
my loved ones, and resentment has me pinned.
Please forgive me as I forgive them—please lift me up.
Praise You for Your grace.
Amen.

God Guarantees

YOU CAN RUN
WITH ENDURANCE

So many godly husbands and wives have gone before you! And today they cheer you on in your efforts to enjoy a righteous marriage. Because so much is at stake—your happiness, My glory—toss aside every weighty hindrance and sin that tickles your fancy. Put distractions away, and I guarantee you that your race will be one of endurance—pure, and full of peace.

FROM HEBREWS 12:1

WARRANTY NOTES: NO ONE RUNS A RACE WITH ROCKS IN HIS SHOES! GET RID, THROUGH FORGIVENESS, OF THE SIN THAT HINDERS YOUR MOVEMENT, AND GO WITH GRACE!

Dear God, I am ready to run with determination. This means I, like the godly husbands and wives before me, put aside the sins that distract me from a clean race. I run toward You today with everything I have.

Amen.

Three

God's
Guarantees
about
Wisdom

God Guarantees

WISDOM BRINGS
SAFETY AND SECURITY

Whoever heeds wise ways—as recorded in My Word and relayed by My Spirit—will know the unspeakable benefits of My safekeeping and fearlessness, whatever married life brings. I promise!

FROM PROVERBS 1:33

WARRANTY NOTES: WE TOO OFTEN SEEK SAFETY AND SECURITY IN THIS SHAKY WORLD IN EXACTLY THE WRONG PLACES—IN SUCH HUMAN SOURCES AS OUR SPOUSES. ONLY GOD CAN PROVIDE SUPERNATURAL CARE.

Dear God,
I need to hide myself in You, not in my spouse.
Only You can protect me, guide me, and fill me with
wisdom for every situation I encounter in life.
Today I take refuge in You alone.
Amen.

God Guarantees

I WILL GIVE WISDOM TO ALL WHO ASK FOR IT

Husband or wife, if you need wisdom today, know that it is just a prayer away. I am as eager to give it as you are to receive it, so ask! I'll make sure you receive a generous portion!

FROM JAMES 1:5

WARRANTY NOTES: NO ANGST REQUIRED—JUST A SIMPLE REQUEST BRINGS ALL THE WISDOM YOU NEED.

Dear God,
Surely I need Your wisdom today.
Please fill me with Your Spirit and guidance,
and be glorified in me as a disciple and
as a husband/wife.
Amen.

God Guarantees

WISDOM BRINGS PLEASURE

Knowledge enlightens: It brings clarity to confusion and lifts burdens from tired backs. In short, it makes you feel better! So seek wisdom at every turn in your marriage—and you'll find pleasure for your soul.

FROM PROVERBS 2:10

WARRANTY NOTES: WHO NEEDS STRIFE AND PAIN? WISDOM IS SO MUCH KINDER TO THE SOUL!

Dear God,
As a spouse, I ask for Your wisdom today.
I want to be the savviest, smartest,
most loving spouse around,
and I can be if I have a good teacher.
I look to You for all I need.
Amen.

God Guarantees

WISDOM GROWS FROM THE INSIDE OUT

I long for you as spouses to know the sweet release wisdom gives—the deep, inner peace that truth imparts. Seek it in Me, and I guarantee you that you will find it.

FROM PSALM 51:6

WARRANTY NOTES: EVERYTHING GOD DOES HE DOES WELL. THIS INCLUDES BLESSING US WITH THE WISDOM WE ASK OF HIM!

Dear God,
I long for Your peace, so I seek Your wisdom.
Thank You for perfect provision.
Amen.

God Guarantees

WISDOM IS FOUND
IN WISE COUNSEL

Children, don't be too proud to learn from others.
If you are struggling in your marriage—or in any
way—seek wisdom from someone who's "been
there, done that" and succeeded. Pride just ignites
arguments; but if you are humble, rest assured that
you and your beloved will also become wise.

FROM PROVERBS 13:10

**WARRANTY NOTES: SOMETIMES OUR BEST
SOURCE OF GOD'S WISDOM IS SOMEONE
WHO IS LIVING BY IT.**

Dear God,
I put aside my pride and ask for Your help today in
discerning who can help me with _____.
As I act in humility, will You meet me
and fill me with Your wisdom?
Amen.

God Guarantees

WISDOM BRINGS
YOU AND ME
CLOSER TOGETHER

My servant Paul prayed for My followers, asking that I would give you the Spirit of wisdom and revelation. He wanted you and Me to be close, as close as spouses—so do I! Request accepted and fulfilled. I guarantee it.

FROM EPHESIANS 1:17; JOHN 16:13

WARRANTY NOTES: WHAT COULD BE BETTER THAN A CONTINUOUS, ABSOLUTELY RELIABLE SOURCE OF SUPERNATURAL WISDOM AND KNOWLEDGE?

Dear God,
Fill me with Your Spirit of wisdom today.
I long to be close to You—and to my spouse—
so please let wisdom do its work in me.
Amen.

God Guarantees

WISDOM POURS FROM A CLOSED MOUTH

Many words usually result in much sin—that you know. Did you know too that the wise spouse who holds his or her tongue makes way for godliness? I guarantee it!

FROM PROVERBS 10:19

WARRANTY NOTES: IT'S WORTH TRYING: SEE IF THE FEWER WORDS YOU SPEAK, THE LESS YOU SIN.

Dear God,
I have shared too many of my thoughts
with my spouse, and they have damaged
him/her and our marriage.
Please forgive me for this and help me to
keep a still, not spouting, tongue.
Thanks for Your help with this
unruly member of my body.
Amen.

God Guarantees

WISE PEOPLE WILL STAND OUT

I declared it to My servant Daniel:"Those who are wise will shine like the brightness of the heavens" (NIV). Your wise living, your godly marriage, will cause you to stand out among the worldly; they will see and be attracted to your righteousness. So shine on, and let Me bless others through you!

FROM DANIEL 12:3

WARRANTY NOTES: WISDOM ISN'T JUST FOR OUR BENEFIT, BUT FOR ALL WHO KNOW US.

Dear God,
Fulfill Your work in me as a spouse,
that I may fulfill my work as Your disciple.
I so long to bring others to Your love and peace.
Amen.

God Guarantees

WISDOM MAKES WAY FOR MINISTRY

Show caution with outsiders; use every opportunity to reach them with My love. As you act wisely—which starts at home, in your marriage and family—your ministry will take effect. I'll make sure your good efforts are not wasted.

FROM COLOSSIANS 4:5; 1 CORINTHIANS 15:58

WARRANTY NOTES: WISDOM IS MORE THAN A GOOD IDEA—IT'S AN ESSENTIAL INGREDIENT OF EFFECTIVE MINISTRY.

Dear God,
Help me to practice Your wisdom
at home with my spouse so I can practice it
in public—to Your glory.
Amen.

Four

G o d ' s

G u a r a n t e e s

a b o u t   H i s

L e a d e r s h i p

God Guarantees

I WILL LEAD
YOU WITH LOVE

Husband and wife, I will tend you with loving care. Those who are struggling or stumbling need not fear; I carry the most vulnerable near My heart. Those with young children will know gentle guidance all along their way.

FROM ISAIAH 40:11

WARRANTY NOTES: GOD CHOSE TO PICTURE HIMSELF NOT AS A DRILL SERGEANT, BUT AS A SHEPHERD. THAT TELLS US ALL WE NEED TO KNOW ABOUT HIS CARE FOR US, AS INDIVIDUALS AND AS SPOUSES.

Dear God,
Please hold me close to Your heart today.
I need exactly what You offer:
shepherding…protection…leading.
Show me Your way and keep me near You.
Amen.

God Guarantees

I WILL LEAD YOU
ON LEVEL GROUND

You and I desire the same things for your married life: that you would experience My unfailing love, rest because of your trust in Me, know My will, and enjoy safety from enemies. In short, that you will walk on clear, smooth paths. Therefore, as you seek these things, expect them! I am ready and eager to provide them—I promise.

FROM PSALM 143:8-10

WARRANTY NOTES: IT'S SO GOOD TO KNOW THAT GOD AND I ARE AFTER THE SAME GOALS!

Dear God,
I am ready and eager to receive all You have for me!
Please show me Your goodness and help my
spouse and me to celebrate it every day.
Amen.

God Guarantees

I LEAD YOU TO ABUNDANCE

Don't fear! I will guide you each and every day. As you serve Me, I will see to your needs: rain when the sun scorches, warmth when cold arrests movement. Your marriage will thrive like a perfectly tended garden, flourishing in all seasons, endlessly showing My glory.

FROM ISAIAH 58:11

WARRANTY NOTES: GOD IS THE SOURCE OF ALL GOOD THINGS—AND HE ALONE CAN SEE US THROUGH THE CHANGING SEASONS OF MARRIAGE.

Dear God,
I'm grateful for Your resources, for mine are dry.
Lord, please fill me with Your Spirit so that I
may flower for You and for my spouse.
Amen.

I AM THE LIGHT IN YOUR DARKNESS

Relax—you and your spouse can't escape My sight or My care. Even if darkness falls heavy around you—in the form of financial troubles, a relentless personal issue, in-law squabbles—know that a shaft of My love will soon brighten your way. In fact, I can and will make darkness shine like day!

FROM PSALM 139:11–12

WARRANTY NOTES: DARKNESS IS FEARSOME ONLY WHEN YOU'RE ALONE IN IT.

Dear God,
Today we lift this nagging problem to You.
We cannot find our way around
or through it, but You can.
Illuminate our darkness and
help us both to glorify You.
Amen.

God Guarantees

I FULFILL MY PURPOSES FOR YOU BOTH

I know you are troubled today. You worry that you have failed your spouse—and Me—too often to know My blessing. Don't take on more than you can carry! Success finds its roots in Me, and as you do your best, I fill in the gaps with My enduring love. I will fulfill every purpose I have for you and your mate; I never abandon the works of My hands.

FROM PSALM 138:8

WARRANTY NOTES: IT'S SO EASY TO FORGET: GOD IS IN CHARGE OF EVERYTHING, EVEN OUR SUCCESS AS A COUPLE. ALL WE HAVE TO OFFER IS OUR BEST EFFORT, AND IT IS ENOUGH.

Dear God, grace has never meant more to me.
You know I long to be a wonderful spouse, yet I stumble.
I lift up our marriage, asking that You continue to "fill in
the gaps." I will do my part and trust You for the rest.
Amen.

God Guarantees

I HAVE SENT A HELPER
TO GUIDE YOU

You are never alone. I have sent My Holy Spirit to accompany, in fact, *abide within,* the two of you. He speaks only truth, only the words I give Him, and I guarantee that He will be a sure guide to you both in every way you need it.

FROM JOHN 16:13

WARRANTY NOTES: WE HAVE A PERFECT TRAINING MANUAL IN THE BIBLE AND ALSO A TUTOR TO CLARIFY EVERY LESSON!

Dear God, I felt pretty alone today, and I'm grateful for Your reminder that You are with me in the closest way possible. It's funny how marriage can feel so lonely sometimes. I rely on Your Spirit to show me all I need to know—especially what I can do to remind my spouse that he/she has my loving companionship whenever it's needed. I praise You for this gift.
Amen.

God Guarantees

THE MYSTERIES
OF LIFE ARE MINE

Husband and wife, I order your steps, ordain your paths, plan your days. Rest in My ability to lead, and I promise to lead well!

FROM PROVERBS 20:24

WARRANTY NOTES: YOU DON'T HAVE TO KNOW IT ALL, BECAUSE GOD DOES.

Dear God,
Thank You for again providing what we
cannot produce: perfect planning.
We rest in it today.
Amen.

God Guarantees

TRUST IS YOUR JOB; GUIDANCE IS MY JOB

Don't try to figure out the hows and whys of your life or your marriage. Don't try to understand everything I am doing. Your job is simple: Let Me be God. Your reward is sweet: I will direct your days!

FROM PROVERBS 3:5–6

WARRANTY NOTES: IT'S A TRUTH WORTH REPEATING: GOD IS IN CHARGE, SO I DON'T HAVE TO BE!

Dear God,
I spend many hours trying to make sense
of tangled threads, disconnected circumstances,
and random occurrences. You call me instead to do
nothing but watch You do the smoothing out.
I praise You, and today I obey!
Amen.

God Guarantees

YOUR LIFE
BELONGS TO ME

Your life—and your marriage—is Mine. Therefore, know that I will make sure that your steps fall where they should. When you question, "This opportunity, this risk, this dream—or that one?" trust Me to get you and your mate from point A to point B, smoothly, faithfully, absolutely.

FROM JEREMIAH 10:23

WARRANTY NOTES: IT ISN'T UP TO US TO BE LEADER AND FOLLOWER. LET US CHOOSE OUR ROLE BEFORE GOD WISELY.

Dear God,
You are God; I am Your disciple.
Lead me in Your light; I follow joyfully.
Amen.

Five

God's

Guarantees

about His

Response to Prayer

God Guarantees

I AM NEAR WHEN
YOU PRAY

I have singled out My people for My special attention. You, therefore, can rest assured that I am close to the couple who seeks me in prayer. You have full-time, instantaneous access to Me whenever you need it. Just call. I am near.

FROM DEUTERONOMY 4:7

WARRANTY NOTES: WE HAVE NOT JUST GOD'S "EAR" WHEN WE CALL TO HIM, BUT HIS WHOLE ATTENTION!

Dear God,
Thank You for this assurance.
As we reach out to You,
we trust that You reach back.
Show us how to glorify You today.
Amen.

God Guarantees

ASK, AND YOU
SHALL RECEIVE

Husband and wife—disciples—know that blessing, forgiveness, guidance, and healing are yours for the asking. I want to hear from you in every circumstance: fear of the future, remorse for failure, longing for leading. Seek Me, and you will find Me—I guarantee it.

FROM 2 CHRONICLES 7:14

WARRANTY NOTES: SOMETIMES GOD IS JUST WAITING TO BE ASKED!

Dear God,
I'm so glad You want to hear my prayers,
because I need to pray! As a wife/husband,
I experience every need listed—fear, remorse, longing—
and I come to You with those burdens today.
Show me Your face and Your ways, and I will honor You.
Amen.

God Guarantees

I WILL TELL YOU
GREAT THINGS

Call to Me with seemingly impossible requests for your marriage and see how I respond: with unexpected, unimaginable, unbelievably great answers! Only I can promise this—and I do.

FROM JEREMIAH 33:3

WARRANTY NOTES: WE CAN IMAGINE SOME PRETTY WONDERFUL THINGS, BUT ONLY GOD CAN PROMISE AND PROVIDE THINGS EVEN BEYOND OUR DREAMING!

Dear God,
I honor You as God today:
as the King of all creation,
full of power and light.
I surrender to Your care today.
Here are my questions;
I await Your perfect answers.
Amen.

God Guarantees

I Am Ready to Save You

Remember the time you were full of distress? Your own resources were empty. You faced a calamity in your marriage without words or wisdom, and you were afraid. Then you called on Me; you remembered that I am gracious and compassionate; you knew I would hear when you prayed. And I saved you! The same is true today. If you or your beloved need saving, just ask. I guarantee I will do it.

FROM PSALM 116:4–7

WARRANTY NOTES: GOD'S FAITHFULNESS YESTERDAY STRENGTHENS MY TRUST IN HIM FOR TOMORROW.

Dear God,
I bring to You a deep concern today: _____.
As You have saved me in the past, please save me today.
You are the only one who can.
Amen.

YOU CAN PRAY TO
ME AS "DAD"

My Son showed you how to address Me: "Our Father in heaven." Did you notice the wording—*Father*? Know that I consider you and your mate no less than My children, My precious family. Come to Me as you would your loving dad, for this is who I am.

FROM MATTHEW 6:9

WARRANTY NOTES: THE KINDNESS OF GOD PROMOTES CONFIDENCE AND PEACE.

Dear God, my Father in heaven,
This is Your daughter/son praising
You for being closer than family
and responding as only a
deeply loving relative can.
Amen.

God Guarantees

PRAYER PROVIDES A SHIELD

Husband or wife, know that I encourage prayers of all kinds. Yes, you can even pray about your tendency to sin. Prayer invites My intervention, so pray…pray…pray. I promise to hear every word of a humble petition and use it to your advantage.

FROM LUKE 22:40

WARRANTY NOTES: NO SUBJECT IS OFF-LIMITS, SO SILENCE TOWARD GOD ISN'T REALLY AN OPTION.

Dear God,
I am tempted today toward _____
in my marriage. Will You deliver me from this evil
that I may serve You and my spouse with love?
I really need You today.
Amen.

God Guarantees

WHEN YOU CAN'T PRAY, THE SPIRIT WILL

I know your weakness. I know that words sometimes fail you. Rest assured that I have provided for
this very situation with My Holy Spirit. When
trouble chokes you—conflict with your spouse
over daily issues, worries for a child's school performance, concern about a relative's health—and
you cannot form your petitions, I promise My
Spirit will. He will use groans even more express-
ive than words, and I will hear…and answer.

FROM ROMANS 8:26

WARRANTY NOTES: GRACE REALLY DOES
COVER EVERY HUMAN NEED. GOD ASKS
ABOUT EVEN THE PRAYERS I MOST NEED TO
PRAY—AND HE ANSWERS!

*Dear God, I have no words today to express my worry
over _____. Thank You for sending Your Spirit
to "fill in the blanks" more effectively than I ever can.*
Amen.

God Guarantees

YOUR VOICE IS A
WELCOME SOUND

Husband and wife, don't let daily cares build a boundary between you and Me. In every need, praise, and concern, call to Me. I promise that your voice is a welcome sound and that I want to hear every word.

FROM 1 THESSALONIANS 5:17–18

WARRANTY NOTES: WE'RE NEVER PESTS TO GOD.

Dear God,
Thank You for never tiring of me but actually inviting me to come at all hours with all needs.
I'm here again, grateful for Your presence in my life.
Please cover each concern with Your guidance and care—and thanks for offering.
Amen.

God Guarantees

I WILL OPEN YOUR EYES TO MY WORK

Know that prayer is more than alerting Me to your needs (which I know already). Prayer is also a reminder to you that I exist and that I care for you. It makes you sensitive to how I am at work in your life and marriage and inspires you to be thankful. So devote yourself to prayer. Be assured that it bears great fruit in your life.

FROM COLOSSIANS 4:2

WARRANTY NOTES: PRAYER HELPS ME IN MYRIAD WAYS, INCLUDING JUST MAKING ME GRATEFUL I HAVE SOMEONE TO PRAY TO!

Dear God,
Thanks for hearing and answering, again and again.
Show me how You are working in me as a spouse
and in us as a couple, that we may praise You.
Amen.

God Guarantees

I PAY CLOSE ATTENTION WHEN YOU PRAY

My eyes are on every move made by My righteous followers. Your concerns about your marriage are My concerns as well. Know that because you embrace My ways and seek My face, I will hear and answer you—I am eager to do so!

FROM 1 PETER 3:12

WARRANTY NOTES: HOLINESS BEATS A PATH TO GOD'S DOOR—AND THE DOOR IS ALWAYS OPEN.

Dear God,
I call to You today with needs—
and gratitude because I know You will meet them.
Amen.

Six

God's

Guarantees

about Your

Abundant Life

God Guarantees

YOU MAY FEED ON MY FAITHFULNESS

When you and your partner trust in Me and try to do good, feasting on My faithfulness, I promise that you will experience My abundance—safe borders, rich pasture, My favor—right where you live.

FROM PSALM 37:3

WARRANTY NOTES: GOD TELLS US THAT WE CAN LITERALLY "FEED" ON HIS FAITHFULNESS. JESUS SAID SOMETHING SIMILAR: "I HAVE FOOD TO EAT OF WHICH YOU DO NOT KNOW.... MY FOOD IS TO DO THE WILL OF HIM WHO SENT ME, AND TO FINISH HIS WORK" (JOHN 4:32, 34, NKJV).

Dear God,
We want the life You offer. Strengthen our trust in You.
May we feast on Your faithfulness so that our lives
bring You glory and show others the way to a deeply
satisfying life in You.
Amen.

God Guarantees

I AM YOUR LIFE

Husband and wife, I always make it your choice: life or death, blessings or curses. Know that I long for you to choose well—to choose Me! You can know no better haven. As you love and serve Me, you have direct access to Me. I invite you to hear My counsel and cling to Me when life's storms blow. I will be your very life, and I will give you all good things in your marriage and family.

FROM DEUTERONOMY 30:19–20

WARRANTY NOTES: CAN WE FIND LIFE ANY-WHERE ELSE? GOD IS THE SOURCE OF ALL GOOD!

Dear God,
I choose You. Today I offer my love and my obedience as evidence of my commitment to You. Thank You for clear counsel and for offering me a safe hiding place.
Lord, I'm so glad I can choose You!
Amen.

God Guarantees

SOUND JUDGMENT
LEADS TO SWEET LIFE

I know that as individuals and as a couple, you
desire safety, security, fearlessness in a fearful world,
and perfect rest. These are all yours as you walk in
My wisdom, using careful discernment and sound
thinking to make your way. Sudden disaster won't
come near you; ruin will flee from you; panic will
be foreign to you. No, the ones who follow Me
enjoy confidence, peace, and abundant life. Come
and take it—I designed it for you!

FROM PROVERBS 3:21–26

**WARRANTY NOTES: THE PREREQUISITE IS
JUST AS IMPORTANT AS THE PROMISE: ONLY
A WISE WALK LEADS TO SMOOTH PATHS.**

*Dear God, I've known too much panic and fear in life
already. If there's a way past them, I'm ready to take it!
Make me a discerning disciple and spouse; help me sort
my thoughts into clear judgment.*

Amen.

God Guarantees

ENDURING SUCCESS
CAN BE YOURS

Witness My servant Hezekiah: He showed the way
to a desirable and fulfilling relationship with Me.
He trusted Me; he clung to Me; he obeyed My
commands; he continued to follow Me—no matter what the circumstance. In return, I was near
him; I gave him success in every undertaking; I
made him famous! Husband and wife, I want you
to enjoy that kind of enduring success.

FROM 2 KINGS 18:5–8

WARRANTY NOTES: SOUNDS LIKE A PLUM
ASSIGNMENT—TRUSTING IN, CLINGING TO,
AND SERVING THE GOD I ALREADY LOVE!

*Dear God, I'm good at the clinging part; I'm not as
good at trusting You no matter what life brings. Help
me to do this the way Hezekiah did. Help me to give
You pleasure. Success I leave in Your hands.*
Amen.

God Guarantees

YOUR DREAMS
CAN COME TRUE

Serving Me really has immeasurable results. As you—individually and as a couple—find your delight in Me, you will see that your cherished desires come to fruition. As you commit your life and times to Me, I will make your holiness a shiny and admirable thing in the sight of all who know you.

FROM PSALM 37:4–6

WARRANTY NOTES: DREAM BIG...A KING IS ON YOUR SIDE.

Dear God,
You know the dreams my spouse and I have:
children, a pleasant and godly home,
ministry to others in Your family.
We commit these dreams—and ourselves—to You.
Make us shine, and find glory in us.
Amen.

God Guarantees

YOUR PRIORITIES SHAPE YOUR FUTURE

Know that as My servants, you are different from the rest of the world. You needn't bear burdens like how you will eat or dress adequately. Unbelievers obsess about these things, but you don't have to—you have Me. Your job is to seek Me first above all earthly concerns; I guarantee that all you need will follow.

FROM MATTHEW 6:31–33

WARRANTY NOTES: OUR EARTHLY RESOURCE IS HEAVENLY!

Dear God,
I hate worrying. It declares my lack of faith,
and I can do better. I commit my way to You,
and I seek Your glory today by just calming down.
I praise You for Your provision.
Amen.

God Guarantees

SATISFACTION IS
MY GIFT TO YOU

Husband and wife, everyone on the earth must eat and drink, work and rest. The difference between My servants and unbelievers is that My followers have access to an unspeakable gift: the ability to enjoy their daily lives. When you find yourself relishing your abundance—your work, your spouse, the fruits of your labor—know that you have received this gift. Embracing My ways leads to gladness of heart...I guarantee it.

FROM ECCLESIASTES 5:18–20

WARRANTY NOTES: LIFE AND WORK CAN BE ABOUT MORE THAN "I OWE, I OWE, SO OFF TO WORK I GO." GOD PROMISES!

Dear God, I am delighted to realize that Your gift is at work in my life. I do enjoy my work, my home, my family. Thank You for this blessing. It makes every day meaningful and satisfying.

Amen.

God Guarantees

LONG LIFE IS IN MY HANDS— AND YOUR CHOICES

Be sure that you—even though you are or will be parents—honor your own parents. This activity actually honors Me and brings you great reward: long life, good life. I promise!

FROM EPHESIANS 6:1–3

WARRANTY NOTES: FAMILY HARMONY MEANS MUCH TO THE LORD—AND TO US.

Dear God,
Help me to find ways to honor my parents.
And help us to be good parents that our
children will find easy to esteem.
I know that we honor You, our Father, in this way.
Amen.

God Guarantees

I HAVE PROVIDED
FOR YOU RICHLY

If you are a wealthy couple, remember to put your trust in Me—the one who dealt you your wealth. Money is uncertain; I am not. Instead of savoring your riches, invest them in good deeds. Be generous, ready to share all the good things I have given you. Remember that I, not things and funds, provide all you need to enjoy life—real life.

FROM 1 TIMOTHY 6:17–19

WARRANTY NOTES: EVEN THE POOREST COUPLE HAS SOMETHING TO SHARE.

Dear God,
I had never thought of my spouse and myself as "rich,"
but I guess we are! We savor all the good things in our
lives that have come from You. Help us find ways to
share even when we don't seem to have any extra—
and by doing so, to honor You.
Amen.

God Guarantees

ABUNDANT LIFE
COMES THROUGH JESUS

Husband and wife, your enemy has evil designs against you. But look at what embracing Jesus brings you: eternal salvation, earthly joy. He is the gate that opens to all you can ask or hope for.

FROM JOHN 10:9–10

WARRANTY NOTES: LIFE "TO THE FULL" COMES ONLY FROM A LOVING FATHER AND HIS SERVANT SON. PRAISE CAN BE OUR ONLY RESPONSE!

Dear God,
Surely those terms sum up all of my wishes
and desires: eternal salvation and earthly joy.
I submit myself to Your keeping today
in hopes of enjoying both.
Amen.

Seven

God's

Guarantees

about Your Becoming

a Good Spouse

God Guarantees

I HAVE MADE YOU ONE

As soon as I created a man and a woman, I ordained a special relationship for them to share. Millennia later, it still holds true: A man and a woman will leave their families to form a new family of one flesh. This unbreakable union is My idea and My gift—I guarantee it.

FROM GENESIS 2:24

WARRANTY NOTES: GOD'S IDEAS ARE ALWAYS GOOD, FULL OF UNEXPECTED BLESSING AND RICHNESS.

Dear God,
We forget sometimes that marriage started in Your mind, that it is indeed a "heavenly" idea. Make us sensitive to all the good You've given in our marriage, and help us to be spouses who bring You glory. We thank You for bringing us together. We do believe, Lord, that we are one!
Amen.

God Guarantees

YOU ARE A DIVINELY DESIGNED HELPER

As Adam surveyed and named all the creatures of the earth, he noticed that he alone was, well, alone. Because of his desire and need, and My intention that he know deep companionship, I created Eve. So I have created you for each other, in special, subtle ways only you will know. That joy is always part of My provision.

FROM GENESIS 2:20

WARRANTY NOTES: GOD PUT NO LESS CARE IN DESIGNING YOU THAN HE DID THE FIRST COUPLE. EXPECT TO FIT EACH OTHER AS NO ONE ELSE COULD.

Dear God,
I rejoice today in Your creation—the certainty that You designed me and my spouse perfectly for each other. Show us how beautifully we "fit," and help us to bring You praise.
Amen.

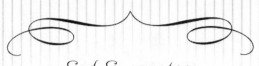

God Guarantees

YOUR MARRIAGE IS CAUSE FOR BLESSING

The man who fears Me and walks in My ways enjoys immeasurable wealth: labor that produces pleasure and prosperity, a wife who produces glorious children, and a rich family life. If you are a husband, you set the tone for your domestic bliss. If you are a wife, you provide for your husband's joy. Trust Me and live fully!

FROM PSALM 128:1–4

WARRANTY NOTES: LET US GIVE GOD SOMETHING HE CAN EASILY BLESS: A GODLY HOME.

Dear God,
I am thankful for the role I play in the family You have
given us. Where I lack as a wife/husband, show me
how to improve. And help us grow in love for each
other and for You that You may bless us.
Amen.

God Guarantees

YOU CAN BRING
HONOR TO YOUR MATE

Wife, if you have noble character, you bring glory to your husband. You are his crown! The same is true of a husband. Act wisely, use sound judgment, discern godly ways from ungodly ones, and you will bring honor to your mate—and to Me.

FROM PROVERBS 12:4

WARRANTY NOTES: AFTER ALL, WHAT IS THE ALTERNATIVE? SCRIPTURE SAYS A DIS-GRACEFUL MATE TEARS DOWN A PARTNER FROM THE BONES OUT!

Dear God,
I want to honor my spouse—and You—
through my behavior. How can I do that today?
Please show me and empower me.
Amen.

God Guarantees

YOUR BELOVED
PROVES MY FAVOR

The person who finds the spouse I've designed finds a treasure: My favor! Whenever you look at your spouse, I promise you are looking at a gift that reflects My love for you.

FROM PROVERBS 18:22

WARRANTY NOTES: REMEMBER THE DAY YOU MET YOUR "INTENDED"? WHEN DID YOU KNOW HE/SHE WAS "THE ONE"? THANK GOD TODAY FOR HIS PERFECT DESIGN AND HIS PLAN THAT BROUGHT YOU TOGETHER.

Dear God,
In each other, You have given us a
blessed sign of Your favor.
We celebrate Your provision in marriage today.
Amen.

God Guarantees

MARITAL HARMONY CAN BE YOURS

I've given you a plan for getting along: submit to one another. Devote yourselves to Me and to one another's good. Nurture and care for each other as you do your own body. Let love and respect be your hallmarks, and you will know sweet harmony. I promise!

FROM EPHESIANS 5:21–23, 28

WARRANTY NOTES: IT'S A GOOD THING GOD DIDN'T DESIGN MARRIAGE WITHOUT ALSO PROVIDING A MODEL TO FOLLOW. WE NEED ALL THE HELP WE CAN GET!

Dear God,
Sometimes love runs dry. It is then especially that I need Your reminders about how to live smoothly with my spouse. Help us to put aside petty conflicts and selfish concerns, and instead look for ways to nourish each other's spirit. To Your glory and our relief!
Amen.

God Guarantees

I Give You Good Examples to Follow

In Paul's letter to Titus, he reminded My followers that older women can teach younger women the marital basics: how to love their families well. This they could do by both example and instruction. Likewise, you have role models in your life to whom you can turn for guidance. Rest assured that becoming a great spouse is within reach as long as you follow the right examples.

FROM TITUS 2:4

WARRANTY NOTES: IF IN DOUBT ABOUT HOW TO HANDLE A MARITAL CONFLICT, LOOK AROUND. SEEK THE COUNSEL OF SOMEONE WHO IS OBVIOUSLY MASTERING THE ART OF HAVING A HAPPY MARRIAGE.

Dear God, thank You for giving us earthly help as well as Your Word to guide us. Help us develop mentoring relationships with those who could lead us best.

Amen.

God Guarantees

ALL THE INGREDIENTS OF A GREAT MARRIAGE ARE WITHIN YOUR GRASP

Self-control. Purity. Responsibility, respect, and honor for My Word. Integrity, soberness, and intelligent speaking: These are the essentials for marriage to not just work but work *well*—for My followers not only to bless Me, but also honor each other. As you work these qualities into your marriage, you can expect that good will follow—I promise.

FROM TITUS 2:5–7

WARRANTY NOTES: WORLDLY EVILS HAVE NO PLACE IN A HOME FILLED WITH THESE SPIRITUAL STRENGTHS.

Dear God, whew—that's a tough list to follow.
But I want to. I entered into marriage to do more than
become a spouse—I want to serve my spouse and You.
Build in me those qualities I lack, to that end.
Amen.

God Guarantees

A SPOUSE WHO FEARS THE LORD IS DEEPLY BLESSED

Charm may get you to the altar, but it won't sustain a relationship. Beauty may attract the eye, but it has no holding power after the vows. But a spouse who follows the Lord will be worthy of praise and receive reward—count on it.

FROM PROVERBS 31:30–31

WARRANTY NOTES: LASTING PLEASURE CAN COME ONLY FROM LASTING QUALITIES SUCH AS GODLY CHARACTER.

Dear God,
I seek to be more than "fun to be around" or attractive.
Develop in me, Lord, the characteristics You most want
to see. I know my spouse will be blessed as a result.
Amen.

YOU CAN BE A TREASURE TO YOUR SPOUSE

Treasure, by definition, is something of unspeakable worth, something highly desired, something to savor. Such is the husband or wife of your youth, if he or she displays reverence for Me and practices My ways. Solomon compared a godly woman with rubies and found the rubies to be worthless; consider then how precious you are to your loved one. Expect your wise behavior to bring blessing to your spouse—it will.

FROM PROVERBS 31:10

WARRANTY NOTES: WHO WOULDN'T LIKE TO BE COMPARED WITH JEWELS AND FOUND MORE DESIRABLE?

Dear God, You have defined my desire: to be of immeasurable value to my spouse. Guide me in the ways that lead to this richness in relationship.
Amen.

Eight

God's
Guarantees
about His
Help

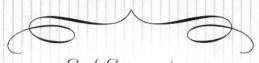

God Guarantees

MY HELP IS MORE VALUABLE THAN MAN'S HELP

When you and your mate look around and cannot find anyone to help you, do not despair. When you come to Me and ask for help, I will always give it. My help will be more timely and valuable than human help. My help will inspire your inmost being and bring both of you joy. When I am your helper, no real harm can come to you. No one can interfere with My rescue efforts.

FROM PSALM 60:11–12

WARRANTY NOTES: THE FIRST PLACE WE SHOULD TURN FOR HELP IS GOD.

*Dear God, we need Your divine help. We are
so overwhelmed by_____. We turn
to You first, right now, and accept Your assistance.
Thank You for helping this marriage!
Amen.*

God Guarantees

I WILL GIVE YOU
A NEW HEART

I will create within you and your beloved a desire to know Me. I will build you up and encourage you both. When the two of you acknowledge Me and call out to Me, I will give you hearts that want to know Me, that are zealous for Me. I will change your hard hearts of stone to hearts that are responsive to Me and My work.

FROM JEREMIAH 24:7; EZEKIEL 11:19

WARRANTY NOTES: GOD IS THE BEST HEART SURGEON OF ALL. HAVE YOU ASKED HIM FOR A TRANSPLANT?

Dear God,
The new life You offer us is precious and miraculous.
We want to give You our hearts of stone and receive
from You soft, obedient, and sensitive hearts. We believe
that You are even now at work on our innermost spirits.
Amen.

God Guarantees

I WILL HELP YOU FIND THE RIGHT WORDS

When you pray, asking to be My messenger, I will give you apt words to speak to people. I know what you will say before you open your mouth, and I know what others, including your mate, need most to hear. Count on Me to make you bold and fearless, and I promise I will put My words in your mouth.

FROM EPHESIANS 6:19; ISAIAH 51:16

WARRANTY NOTES: WHEN YOU DON'T KNOW WHAT TO SAY, DON'T PANIC, BUT PRAY.

Dear God,
From this moment on, enable me to fearlessly speak the
words You give me. I want to be Your messenger to the
people around me (and especially my spouse!).
They desperately need You. Thank You for standing
beside me and my mate when we talk to others.
Amen.

God Guarantees

I HAVE CHOSEN THE WEAK AND FOOLISH

When I choose people to serve Me, I don't necessarily choose those who are wise, influential, or noble by human standards. Instead, I choose the foolish things of this world to shame the wise, and I choose the weak things of this world to shame the strong. I choose couples like you, humble and weak, so that the world cannot give credit to anyone other than Me for the good things you do.

FROM 1 CORINTHIANS 1:26–29

WARRANTY NOTES: GOD DOES HIS BEST WORK IN THE PEOPLE WHO NEED HIM MOST. FIRST CORINTHIANS 1:25 SAYS, "THE FOOLISHNESS OF GOD IS WISER THAN MEN, AND THE WEAKNESS OF GOD IS STRONGER THAN MEN."

Dear God, I often feel foolish and weak. Thank You for Your promise that You can best use those of us with limitations. My mate and I will rely on Your divine help.

Amen.

God Guarantees

You Can Come Boldly to My Throne for Help

When you become dismayed by various temptations, remember that I, Jesus, can sympathize with your weaknesses. In fact, I was tempted in all the same ways that you and your spouse are tempted. Yet I did not sin. This means that you can approach My throne with confidence, knowing I will gladly give you mercy and grace to help you anytime.

FROM HEBREWS 4:15–16

WARRANTY NOTES: BEING SORELY TEMPTED IS NOT THE SAME AS SINNING. JESUS WANTS YOU BOTH TO COME TO HIM FOR HELP, UNASHAMED (HEBREWS 2:17).

Dear God, how wonderful and reassuring it is to know that You promise mercy and grace when we are overcome by temptations. We accept Your wonderful invitation and ask You right now to help us in our battles against temptation and sin. Amen.

God Guarantees

I WILL GIVE
YOU STRENGTH

Husbands and wives, when you feel weakest in your marriage, put your hope in Me. Wait before Me, and I will supernaturally renew your strength. Before too long, you will feel as if you can soar on wings like an eagle. You will run and not grow weary; you will walk and not grow faint.

FROM ISAIAH 40:31

WARRANTY NOTES: THE HEBREW WORD FOR "RENEW" COULD ALSO BE TRANSLATED AS "EXCHANGE." GOD INVITES YOU TO EXCHANGE YOUR WEAKNESS FOR HIS STRENGTH.

*Dear God, I believe that when I am weak, You are able
to give me supernatural strength, allowing me to
persevere in this life. All my hope is in You.
I wait quietly before You, offering my weakness to You,
ready to receive Your renewing power.
Amen.*

God Guarantees

NOTHING IS
IMPOSSIBLE FOR ME

When you or your spouse need My help to do something that seems impossible, you can rest assured that for Me it is not impossible at all. I can do anything I choose to do in your marriage or through your marriage, because what is totally impossible for ordinary man is completely possible with Me.

FROM LUKE 1:37

WARRANTY NOTES: JESUS SAID THAT IF WE REMAIN IN HIM, WE CAN ACCOMPLISH MUCH. BUT APART FROM HIM, WE CAN DO NOTHING (JOHN 15:5).

Dear God, so many things are impossible for me. But I believe that You can do anything, including
_____. *I agree with Jeremiah, who said, "There is nothing too hard for You" (Jeremiah 32:17, NKJV).*
Amen.

God Guarantees

I WILL KEEP YOU FROM FALLING

I am the only God, and I am your Savior. I am committed to keeping sin out of your marriage. I will walk beside you to steady you. I am powerful enough to support and sustain you. You can be confident that I will purify you and will someday joyfully escort you into My glorious presence.

FROM JUDE 1:24–25

WARRANTY NOTES: WHEN WE ARE TEMPTED, GOD WANTS US TO RUN TO HIM FOR HELP, NOT AWAY FROM HIM IN SHAME.

Dear God,
When temptations try to trip me up, I'm counting on
You to help me keep my balance and stand firm.
Thank You for the reassurance that if I ask,
You will help me. I don't have to fall.
Amen.

God Guarantees

FROM YOUR BIRTH I
HAVE BEEN YOUR HELP

Do you realize that from the very moment of both your and your mate's birth, I was your God? Even while each of you nursed at your mother's breast, I caused you to trust in Me. To this day, I will never be far from either of you when trouble is near. When there is no one else to help, I stand ready.

FROM PSALM 22:9–11

WARRANTY NOTES: ALL OF US COME INTO THE WORLD HELPLESS AND COMPLETELY DEPENDENT ON OUR MOTHERS. GOD WANTS US TO SEE THAT, IN THE SAME WAY, WE CONTINUE TO BE TOTALLY HELPLESS AND NEEDY FOR HIM, EVEN AFTER WE ARE GROWN.

Dear God, it's amazing to think that from the moment
of my birth Your hand has been upon me. I trusted in
You before I knew what I was doing. Even now I
depend on You, like a baby depends on its mother.
Amen.

Nine

God's Guarantees about Your Family

God Guarantees

YOU WORSHIP
THE ONLY GOD

You can be certain that I am the only true God!
As a family who worships Me, you can know for
certain that you're not making a big mistake. I'm
the one and only God of the universe, the only
God who possesses the power to hurt My enemies
and to heal those who love Me. No one can take
your family from My hand.

FROM DEUTERONOMY 32:39

WARRANTY NOTES: GOD WANTS US TO LIVE IN
FULL CONFIDENCE THAT HE ALONE IS SOV-
EREIGN AND ALL-POWERFUL.

Dear God,
I believe that You alone are God and that my family is
intimate with the one and only God of the universe!
This is amazing to me. I trust all my hopes for my
family to Your sovereign power.
Amen.

God Guarantees

YOUR GODLINESS WILL BLESS YOUR CHILDREN

Know that your righteous behavior does more than set a good example for your children; it opens up a treasure of blessing for them. I guarantee that a godly parent creates good gifts for his or her children.

FROM PROVERBS 20:7

WARRANTY NOTES: THE GIFT THAT KEEPS ON GIVING: HOLINESS.

Dear God,
My spouse and I have known
the fulfillment of following You.
I praise You that I can expect to see goodness
result in the lives of my children as well.
It is more than worth it to serve You.
Amen.

God Guarantees

YOUR GENEROSITY MEANS PROVISION FOR YOUR CHILDREN

When I delight in a parent—a parent who obeys Me—I arrange his steps in safe places. I catch him when he stumbles; I uphold him when he falls; I see to the welfare of his children. Such a person shows his devotion to Me by his generosity and giving, and his children know My blessing as a result.

FROM PSALM 37:23–26

WARRANTY NOTES: IF YOU WANT TO FEEL SURE ABOUT YOUR CHILDREN'S FUTURE, WALK WITH GOD.

Dear God, I am grateful that You care more about our family than even my spouse and I do. And I praise You for the trickle-down effect of following You—that You'll see to my children's needs as well as to ours. I praise You and commit all of us to You.

Amen.

God Guarantees

YOUR FAMILY FINDS SAFE REFUGE IN YOUR GODLINESS

The parent who fears Me is more than smart; he is absolutely secure from every violent, evil force. And his fortress will always be big enough to include his family—I promise.

FROM PROVERBS 14:26

WARRANTY NOTES: WHAT IS A PARENT'S NUMBER-ONE DESIRE FOR HIS CHILD? WHAT DOES GOD PROMISE WILL RESULT FROM GODLY LIVING? IT'S THE SAME THING: SAFETY.

Dear God,
I'm grateful that You promise to shield my children,
and I'm grateful that the best thing my spouse and
I can do is follow You.
It's a pleasure!
Amen.

God Guarantees

I WILL NEVER FORSAKE YOUR FAMILY

I am more than friend; I am Savior and stronghold for the family of the parents who serve Me. My faithfulness inspires lifelong trust, and I never forget, neglect, or forsake those who follow Me. I guarantee it!

FROM PSALM 9:9–10

WARRANTY NOTES: IT'S THE ULTIMATE LIFE INSURANCE—FROM AN ETERNALLY FAITHFUL SOURCE.

Dear God,
It gives me such peace to know
that You are committed to my family.
It strengthens our commitment as spouses
and parents to please and serve You
and model Your ways to our children.
Amen.

God Guarantees

CHILDREN ARE A
BLESSING FROM ME

Can you believe that I want to give you the best of all gifts? I do, and children are one of them. Know that I design them especially for you and your strengths. The man or woman with many children exhibits My favor.

FROM PSALM 127:3–5

WARRANTY NOTES: SEE YOUR FAMILY FOR EXACTLY WHAT IT IS—SOMETHING CREATED ESPECIALLY FOR YOU AND FOR GOD'S GLORY.

Dear God,
Thank You for these gifts from Your hand.
Sometimes in the busyness of the day I forget
that each of my children was God-ordained.
Thank You for the blessing they and my spouse
bring daily, just by being my family.
Amen.

God Guarantees

I CREATED YOU
TO PROCREATE

After I made man and woman, I gave them a unique command: to make more of themselves. Your family offers a sign of both My blessing and My empowerment, for children come only by My design.

FROM GENESIS 1:28; PSALM 139:13

WARRANTY NOTES: CHILDREN ARE NEVER AN "ACCIDENT" IN GOD'S EYES.

Dear God,
Make my spouse and me good guides
for all You have planned to do
in and through our children.
Help us to show them the
perfect path—following You.
Amen.

God Guarantees

MY SALVATION BELONGS TO YOUR CHILDREN TOO

I brought My message of eternal life to adults, but I assure you it is for your children too. Anyone—everyone—who seeks salvation through Jesus will have it. I promise!

FROM ACTS 2:39

WARRANTY NOTES: GOD SEES CHILDREN AS WORTHY RECEPTACLES FOR HIS GIFTS—PRAISE HIM!

Dear God,
Thank You for designing salvation even in kid sizes.
Help us as spouses and parents to model why it is
the most important choice they can make.
Amen.

God Guarantees

YOUR CHILDREN CAN SERVE ME

Samuel, the son I gave the mourning Hannah, served Me from a young age in the temple. Your child is endowed with this ability as well. There is no age limit on who can glorify Me; through your guidance, your child can walk worthy of My kingdom. I guarantee it.

FROM 1 SAMUEL 2:11

WARRANTY NOTES: YET ANOTHER HABIT THAT'S WORTH STARTING YOUNG: SERVING THE LORD GOD!

Dear God,
I long for my children to be pleasing servants to You,
even at their young ages. Please help us as parents to
recognize opportunities to draw them to You and show
them how to honor You.
Amen.

God Guarantees

I'M A GOOD FATHER

Just as you know the difference between bread and stones, fish and snakes; just as you choose only good gifts for your children, so do I. If you know how to love them skillfully and faithfully, you can count on the fact that I do too—only immeasurably more! Expect My perfect care in their lives and yours.

FROM MATTHEW 7:9–11

WARRANTY NOTES: PARENTAL LOVE STARTED WITH—AND FINDS ITS FULFILLMENT IN—GOD.

Dear God,
We want to express Your rich love
between ourselves as spouses and to our
children as their parents.
Empower us to love the way You do.
Nothing less will do.
Amen.

Ten

God's Guarantees about Your Purity and Faithfulness

THE MARRIAGE BED IS A GOOD THING

Husband and wife, honor your marriage covenant. If you want a richly fulfilled union, one that is blessed by My hand, be completely faithful to one another. I promise to judge only those who earn My judgment—the adulterer and the sexually immoral.

FROM HEBREWS 13:4

WARRANTY NOTES: WHEN WE HONOR OUR COMMITMENT TO ONE ANOTHER, WE AFFIRM OUR COMMITMENT TO GOD.

Dear God,
I'm so grateful for my spouse and all the
ways You've filled our lives with love.
I promise to be faithful to him/her and thus
be faithful to You as well. I watch for Your blessing!
Amen.

God Guarantees

I EMPOWER YOUR FAITHFULNESS

I've given you another reason to love Me—I preserve those who are faithful. The proud repel Me, but those who humbly keep their commitments—including those to their spouses—I strengthen for more good works.

FROM PSALM 31:23

WARRANTY NOTES: DOING GOOD MULTIPLIES ITSELF.

Dear God,
I admit that my eye wanders at times, but Your Word
and Your Spirit draw me back to my spouse.
I renew my commitment to him/her today.
I lean on Your strength to be perfectly faithful,
in thought and action, to this person
You chose so wisely for me.
Amen.

God Guarantees

I WILL GIVE LIFELONG BLESSING TO THE FAITHFUL

You know I love the ones who make a commitment and keep it, no matter how much they're tested. I will never forsake the ones who cling to Me and express their faithfulness in all things, including their marriages. Such persons will enjoy My companionship and blessing throughout life.

FROM PSALM 37:28–29

WARRANTY NOTES: GOD'S RIGHTEOUS ONES STAND OUT BECAUSE THEY STAND UP FOR THEIR COMMITMENTS. THEY EXPERIENCE GOD'S ABUNDANCE.

Dear God,
Thank You for my spouse and his/her commitment to
me. I promise that I will return that fidelity of heart
and soul for as long as I live—with Your help.
Amen.

God Guarantees

I HEAR THE PRAYERS
OF THE PURE

How you call on Me determines how I answer. If you call from a pure heart—one that is faithful and true in all its ways—I will hear and respond. If you call out from a sinful place you have come to adore, I won't hear you at all. Purity paves the way to My heart.

FROM PROVERBS 15:29

WARRANTY NOTES: PURITY IS MORE THAN A GOOD IDEA.

Dear God,
I want You to hear my prayers.
So I pursue purity in all its forms: in my giving,
in my serving, in my faithfulness to my spouse.
Bless our marriage as we seek
to follow You in holiness.
Amen.

God Guarantees

I WILL USE YOUR EXAMPLE

Show your faithfulness to Me in love, in speech, in faith, in life, and in purity. Such an example of godly behavior won't be wasted; it will earn you respect and influence. As you show your diligence in My ways—including in your marital vows—I will use you in My service.

FROM 1 TIMOTHY 4:12, 16

WARRANTY NOTES: GOD CAN ALWAYS USE A MAN OR WOMAN WHO IS A MODEL OF FIDELITY.

Dear God,
I long to please You, to be used by You.
I offer You my faithfulness and ask You to
empower it for Your glory and service.
Amen.

God Guarantees

YOUR PURITY IMPACTS YOUR SPOUSE

Your holy behavior does more than bless you and honor Me; it may affect your spouse for eternity. A pure, reverent life speaks louder than many a preached word! I promise to bless such activity.

FROM 1 PETER 3:1–2

WARRANTY NOTES: IF YOU WANT TO SEE SPIRITUAL DEVELOPMENT IN YOUR SPOUSE, START BY LIVING A GODLY LIFE YOURSELF.

Dear God,
Here is an area where I surely fail often.
Renew in me the ability to live such a pure
and reverent life—for You and for my spouse—
that I can become a tool in Your hands.
Amen.

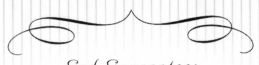

God Guarantees

MY WORD MAKES YOU PURE

Purity comes about in your life as you live according to My Word. My Word alerts you to potential speed bumps and dangerous detours on the road to holiness. Heed it, and it will save you. Ignore it, and encounter many sad side trips. Know that purity can result only from a life lived close to Me.

FROM PSALM 119:9–10

WARRANTY NOTES: FIDELITY SPRINGS FROM A GOD-INFORMED LIFE. SOAK YOURSELF IN HIS WORD AND KNOW THE FREEDOM OF FAITHFULNESS!

Dear God,
Like the young man who wrote Psalm 119,
I long to immerse myself in Your commands.
I see that they are a shield of safety and blessing for me
and for my marriage. Clothe me today in Your Word.
Amen.

God Guarantees

YOUR HOPE IN ME PURIFIES YOU

My children, now that you are My very own, you know what you have to look forward to: becoming just like Jesus in all His beauty and sinlessness. When you finally, physically see Him, you will be as He is: perfect, shining in holiness. Everyone who anticipates this change does what he can now, on earth; he purifies himself, puts sin aside. When you do this, you reveal My work and presence in your life. Know that I see your effort and honor it..

FROM 1 JOHN 3:2–3

WARRANTY NOTES: ONLY GOD CAN MAKE US ENTIRELY SINLESS, BUT WE CAN ENHANCE THE CLEANSING PROCESS (2 CORINTHIANS 7:1)!

Dear God, I want not only to cooperate with You in the ways You are making me like Jesus—I want to do all I can this side of heaven. Show me ways I can be more pure.

Amen.

God Guarantees

THE FAITHFUL ENJOY LIGHT, JOY, AND PROTECTION

Love Me; hate evil. Show faithfulness in your work, in your marriage, and in your servanthood. The result? Deliverance from the wicked and a life washed in light and joy—I guarantee it.

FROM PSALM 97:10–11

WARRANTY NOTES: FIDELITY PAYS OFF NOT JUST IN MARRIAGE, BUT ALSO IN ALL OF LIFE.

Dear God,
What a glorious invitation:
Following You leads to a life
marked by Your love.
I accept!
Amen.

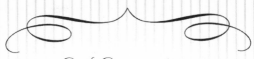

God Guarantees

I AM FAITHFUL TO HELP
YOU UNTIL THE END

Just as the apostle Paul prayed, I am at work in you, sanctifying every part, working to keep you blameless until the coming of My Son. Because I called you, I will complete you—rest assured that I am faithful from beginning to end.

FROM 1 THESSALONIANS 5:23–24

WARRANTY NOTES: GOD CALLS US TO BE AS HE IS: PERFECTLY PURE, FOREVER FAITHFUL.

Dear God,
Thank You for laboring to make
me all You know I can be.
I want to exude Your purity and
fidelity in every aspect of my life,
so come and be glorified in me.
I commit my life into Your hands.
Amen.

Eleven

God's

Guarantees

about Your

Spiritual Strength

You're Strong Even When You're Weak

Remember how My servant Paul struggled with a "thorn" in his flesh? I know you know what that feels like; you've felt the pangs in your own life and in your marriage. But know also, as Paul did, that weakness is an opportunity for My strength to show. Don't be ashamed of your spiritual frailty; My abundance will supply what you need.

FROM 2 CORINTHIANS 12:7–10

WARRANTY NOTES: THINK ABOUT IT: IF WE WERE PERFECTLY STRONG ON OUR OWN, WE WOULD HAVE NO NEED FOR GOD. BECAUSE WE'RE WEAK, WE RELY ON THE STRONG— AND HE IS GLORIFIED!

Dear God,
Your strength is my greatest comfort today. My own
thorn threatens to fester, but I trust You to overcome
where I cannot. Glory to You for Your many gifts!
Amen.

I PROVIDE STRENGTH FOR MY SERVICE

Though I allowed My Son to be crucified in weakness, I made sure power was apparent soon after: *He lived and lives!* In the same way, though your own strength fails often, My power enlivens you again and again. Rest assured that strength for My service—in your marriage, family, and other close relationships—will always be yours.

FROM 2 CORINTHIANS 13:4

WARRANTY NOTES: GOD WANTS OUR SERVICE EVEN MORE THAN WE LONG TO SERVE HIM; THEREFORE, WE CAN EXPECT HIM TO EMPOWER US.

Dear God, the example of Your Son coming to life again is a powerful one for me today. Sometimes I feel completely drained of strength—yet marriage calls for endless energy. I rely on Your power where my own is tapped out. Thank You for perfect supply.

Amen.

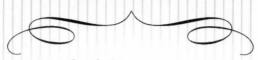

God Guarantees

I STRENGTHEN COMMITTED HEARTS

I am watching over every person on the earth, searching for the hearts that belong to Me. As you give Me your whole loyalty and self, I give even more strength to accomplish My works in your marriage.

FROM 2 CHRONICLES 16:9

WARRANTY NOTES: STRENGTH TO SERVE WELL IN MARRIAGE ARISES FROM A HEART FULLY COMMITTED TO GOD AND SPOUSE.

Dear God,
Here is my heart; I want it to be all Yours.
Then love can come from it for my spouse,
my family, my colleagues, even my enemies.
Amen.

God Guarantees

BECAUSE YOU ARE MINE, I WILL HELP YOU

You are My servant, so I am your help. Don't let fear cut you off from the truth! I am with you; I will help you; I will uphold you with My righteous right hand. Count on it.

FROM ISAIAH 41:9–10

WARRANTY NOTES: COULD WE EXPECT GOD'S COMMITMENT TO US TO BE ANY LESS THAN PERFECT?

Dear God,
I am Yours, which is a rich truth
to immerse myself in today.
I commit the cares of my marriage into Your keeping,
and I watch for Your hand of deliverance.
Amen.

God Guarantees

I AM THE SOURCE OF YOUR CONFIDENCE

I can empower you to do more than you imagine possible; I can make your feet as swift as a deer's so that you may scale the heights! Be confident that I am with you and will enable you to do all good things, including love your beloved spouse richly.

FROM HABAKKUK 3:19

WARRANTY NOTES: GOD WANTS ME TO MOVE SMOOTHLY AND SPEEDILY AS I FOLLOW HIM DOWN THE NARROW WAY.

Dear God,
Sometimes I stumble on this long road of marriage.
Make my feet as the deer's;
make my heart light and agile.
Thank You for showing Your commitment
to me as I show mine to my spouse.
Amen.

God Guarantees

YOU CAN DO *ANYTHING* IN ME

There is no difficult task, no conflicted relationship, no dire circumstance that you can't handle through My strength. I have power, and I am glad to share it with you.

FROM PHILIPPIANS 4:13

WARRANTY NOTES: EVEN THE TOUGHEST DAY IN YOUR MARRIAGE IS NO MATCH FOR GOD'S STRENGTH.

Dear God,
I exchange my weakness today for Your strength.
Thank You for not hoarding Your power,
but offering it to those who need it for Your service.
Amen.

God Guarantees

I WILL NEVER FAIL YOU

You know well your own frailty, physically and spiritually. But by now you also know My strength, that I sustain those who rely on Me. Those couples who pull away from Me know no help; those who cling to Me experience My flawless faithfulness. They have many tales of deliverance to share with others. Remember, I am the only one who will never fail you!

FROM PSALM 73:26–28

WARRANTY NOTES: THAT'S WHAT I CALL HOPE: GOD IS ON MY SIDE!

Dear God,
We want to be one of those couples who shines with
Your blessing. Your faithfulness, we know, is the key.
Strengthen our service to You and to each other.
Thank You for delivering us time and again.
Amen.

I WILL RESCUE
YOU FROM EVIL

Paul recorded the way I was with him through testings and trials; so I am with every heart that serves Me. As I stood by his side against accusers and threats and fear, so I will stand at yours and rescue you. Count on Me to strengthen you for every good work in life and marriage, all the way to My kingdom.

FROM 2 TIMOTHY 4:17–18

WARRANTY NOTES: AREN'T YOU GLAD GOD DOESN'T STOP HALFWAY AND SAY, "YOU'RE ON YOUR OWN"?

Dear God,
Evil is a fearful thing.
Thank You for giving me confidence in the face of it.
Deliver us individually and as a couple from the
evil one, that we may give You glory.
Amen.

God Guarantees

YOU DISPLAY
MY STRENGTH

It is your choice: You can reveal My strength or you can exude your own weakness. You know that I am slow to anger, rich in love and forgiveness. By acting the same way—by being patient with your spouse, ready to speak kind words and offer forgiveness—you put My strength on display for the world to see.

FROM NUMBERS 14:17–18

WARRANTY NOTES: IF YOU'RE GOING TO PUT ON A SHOW, MAKE IT A GOOD ONE!

Dear God,
I want my life to show not my weakness, but Your power. I know this can occur only through my submission to Your will and ways. Here I am, Lord. Please work in and through me.
Amen.

God Guarantees

MY STRENGTH
GIVES YOU PEACE

Because I am on My throne, you are safe in My
strength. Because My kingdom has no end, your
security is everlasting. Know that I give strength to
those who are Mine; I bless My people with peace.

FROM PSALM 29:10–11

WARRANTY NOTES: WE TRUST IN A SAVIOR
AND KING. CAN WE LACK ANYTHING?

Dear God,
I praise You today for Your holiness,
Your vastness, Your faithfulness to the weak
mortals in Your care. Thank You for being, in our
marriage, a beacon of strength and peace.
Amen.

CERTIFICATE OF MOTHERHOOD

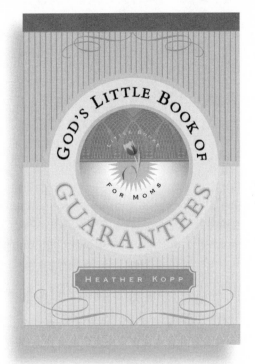

It's official. You're a mom. But what guarantees that you can meet the daunting challenges of family life unfolding just ahead? Plenty! In the fine print of these enduring Warranty Notes is your spiritual insurance policy for motherhood. Discover God's promise of partnership and a flush benefits package for those who parent. Carry it. Share it. Build on it securely. Signed, sealed, delivered—it's yours!

ISBN 1-59052-023-8

FOR WIVES WHO STAY...EVEN WHEN IT HURTS.

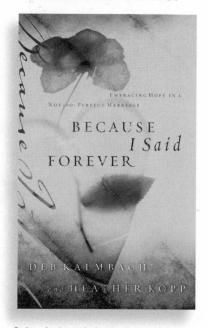

Maybe you feel a little jaded. You've read Christian marriage books but can't identify. The problems seem trivial, the solutions unrealistic. This book is different. Guided by scriptural principles, the authors provide life-tested advice and solid spiritual support for a wife making the tough choice to stay in a difficult marriage. This resource will help you find wisdom in nurturing your marriage, patience in honoring your husband, and the courage to keep reaching for God's best each day.

ISBN 1-57673-852-3